D1712482

Loud Sounds, Soft Sounds

Patty Whitehouse

Rourke
Publishing LLC
Vero Beach, Florida 32964

www.rourkepublishing.com

PHOTO CREDITS: © David and Patricia Armentrout: pages 4, 5, 6, 7, 10, 11, 14, 15, 18, 20; © Craig Lopetz: pages 8, 16, 19; © Lynn Stone: page 12; © constructionphotographs.com: page 13; © Karen Phillips: page 21; © Zoe Yau: page 17

Editor: Robert Stengard-Olliges

Cover and interior design by Nicola Stratford

Library of Congress Cataloging-in-Publication Data

Whitehouse, Patricia, 1958-
  Loud sounds, soft sounds / Patty Whitehouse.
     p. cm. -- (Construction forces)
  Includes index.
  ISBN 1-60044-191-2 (hardcover)
  ISBN 1-59515-552-X (softcover)
1. Machinery--Sounds--Juvenile literatue. 2. Noise--Juvenile literature.
3. Telecommunication--Juvenile literature. 4. Sound--Juvenile literature.
5. Building sites--Juvenile literature. I. Title. II. Series: Whitehouse,
Patricia, 1958- Construction forces.
  TJ153.W625 2007
  534--dc22
                              2006008860

Printed in the USA

CG/CG

Rourke Publishing

www.rourkepublishing.com – sales@rourkepublishing.com
Post Office Box 3328, Vero Beach, FL 32964
1-800-394-7055

Table of Contents

Construction Site Sounds

This is a **construction site**. It gets very noisy here.

Trucks and **machines** make sounds. People make sounds, too.

Making and Hearing Sounds

Sounds are made when something **vibrates**. Most things vibrate too quickly to see.

Sounds travel in waves. The sound from the truck travels in waves to our ears.

Loud Sounds

Some sounds at the construction site are loud. They can be heard far away.

Driller

Drillers make loud sounds. The sound travels in the air and through the ground.

Soft Sounds

Some construction sounds are soft. A hand saw makes a soft sound.

Finishers are very quiet workers. The noise from the trowel does not travel far.

High Sounds

A circular saw makes a screeching sound. It has a high pitch.

Trucks go *beep-beep-beep* when they back up. The beep has a high pitch, too.

Low Sounds

A digger makes a rumbling sound as it digs. Its **motor** has a low pitch.

Big trucks have big motors. Big motors have a low pitch when they move slowly.

Keep It Quiet!

Construction site sounds sometimes get too loud. The sounds are called **noise pollution**.

Some construction sites put up sound **barriers**. They help stop the sounds from going too far.

Keeping Sound Out

Workers close to loud sounds wear ear muffs. Ear muffs keep the sound out of their ears.

Some buildings need to be very quiet. These tiles can help **soundproof** the rooms.

People and Sound

People need to talk about the work at a construction site. Some workers use walkie-talkies.

    Some people use cell phones at a construction site.
Then they can work and talk.

Try It!

Which of these are soft sounds? Which are loud sounds?

GLOSSARY

construction site (kuhn STRUHKT shun SITE): a place where workers build

barrier (BA ree ur): a wall that stops sound

machine (muh SHEEN): something that uses energy to help people work

motor (MOH tur): an engine that makes something move

noise pollution (NOIZ puh LOO shuhn): filling the air with unwanted noise

soundproof (SOUND PROOF): keeping sound out

vibrate (VYE brate): fast back-and-forth movement that makes sound

INDEX

FURTHER READING

Kilby, Don. *At a Construction Site.* Kids Can Press, 2003.
Parker, Steve. *Sound*. Chelsea House Publishers, 2005.
Pettigrew, Mark. *Music and Sound.* Stargazer Books, 2004.

WEBSITES TO VISIT

http://library.thinkquest.org/5116/sound.htm
http://science.howstuffworks.com/engineering-channel.htm
http://www.bobthebuilder.com/usa/index.html

ABOUT THE AUTHOR

Patty Whitehouse has been a teacher for 17 years. She is currently a Lead Science teacher in Chicago, where she lives with her husband and two teenage children. She is the author of more than 100 books about science for children.